Meet Me in HR
Finding Hope in Unemployment

. . . .

NADINE SCHOFIELD

The word which God has written on the brow of every man is Hope.

VICTOR HUGO, Les Misérables

PRESS

DEDICATION

I dedicate this book to my husband, Mark, who has faithfully, joyfully, and steadfastly walked the path of unemployment, and to our children, Joel and Jenna.

It is with gratitude that I would also like to acknowledge the hard work and tenacity of Christopher Jacobsen to read, correct, and improve my manuscript with his editing skills.

Lastly, I would like to thank my friend Deborah Sovinee for her creative talents to design the cover as one who has also experienced the unemployment journey. She recounts how she felt, "suddenly losing my job, after 24 years as a Senior Exhibit Designer for a museum, was a shock to my system. I felt betrayed by an institution I had loved. What I could not have imagined is that my life would transform in many positive ways. The idea for the cover of this book came to me in the middle of the night after I read Nadine's first chapter draft. It was so healing to sit down and let it flow out of me. So, I see myself as the first one to be healed by this story."

CONTENTS

Introduction.. vii

1. The Day.. 13

2. God's Provision 21

3. The New Norm 29

4. Wisdom From Some Old Books 38

5. The Roller Coaster 50

6. The Scarlet "U" 62

7. Merry Heart Moments 69

8. Ten Truths for the Journey.................... 77

9. If I Ran the Zoo 86

10. A Wife's Reflections 95

11. Thirty Days to Meditate...................... 102

12. The Beat Goes On; It's a Waiting Game..... 109

End Notes 119

Introduction

*G*rowing up I never really liked the game musical chairs. The exuberant amount of energy expended running around and around the chairs was fun, but there also was a level of uncomfortable anticipation lurching forward to the next chair waiting for the music to stop so you could sit down and not be left out. My dislike for this game centered on being eliminated, feeling the sense of loss that you were cast out. Presently, many of us are finding ourselves without that "available chair" as we face the loss of our jobs in this time of economic downturn, and in fact 14 million of us have found ourselves with no chair to sit in with the unemployment rate in the United States hovering at 9 percent.

Each of these 14 million people has a story, an

individual journey through the troubled waters of unemployment. A friend's husband lost his job this year along with 4,500 others at his company, happening all in one day! Imagine going along in life knowing you have a job and then in one day all is reversed. Recently another friend's husband at age 60 was let go from his company and he just earned a sales award the month before. Along with shock and disbelief there is a feeling that this does not make sense, a daze of confusion and helplessness.

In the numbers of people who find themselves unemployed, there are the middle aged, middle class, the executives, the hourly wage earners, the older unemployed, the educated and not so educated, and even the young college graduates desiring to find meaningful employment in their area of interest and study. We all come from a variety of backgrounds but all have one thing in common as stated by Rich Lowry an editor of *National Review*, "We were built to work. When we want to and can't, it is an assault on our very personhood."[1]

At the beginning of 2011 my husband Mark lost

his job and started his journey of being unemployed. We entered these uncharted waters with no preparation or guidebook to lead the way. This has been an amazing, new, growing experience for both of us, and certainly something we had never anticipated. As I tell our story it is our desire that others would be encouraged and can grab on to hope in their own situations as well. We believe that with the staggering numbers of unemployed our experience is similar to others and is echoed across the land by so many.

My husband has been employed for the last 32 years, and was passionate about the mission of the two companies he worked at and for people who worked there. He is a "people and passion" person and delights in building a team, and encouraging people to work to their strengths. At his most recent job, he was tasked with building a business unit that was strongly customer focused within the larger company and involved product development, marketing and delivery. In the ten years he was at this company this part of the business under his leadership grew three-fold. For the past several years, however, the company began to make a subtle slow change where process and procedure was beginning to be valued more than people and passion. His experience was a bit like the proverbial frog put in cool water and then placed on the heat so the water gradually turned warm and then finally boiled, but the frog was unaware because the change was insidious. Mark realized the water was boiling on the day the big announcement was made that "we are going to reorganize", taking apart the team that Mark had built.

The cry from upper management was "we want to grow our company" and this was the way they envisioned it should be done, after all that is what the organizational development experts advised. Somehow, the experts disregarded the bottom line truth that Mark's business unit grew three-fold while the rest of the company progressed at a fraction of that rate. It was hard to see what he spent ten years building being taken apart with the swipe of a pen. But he still had a job as they pegged him in a different place on the organizational chart as Division Manager of Training Product Development, and for this we were thankful. However, seven months after this reorganization was a different story, the news that his job was eliminated.

My husband and I have a strong faith in God. We realize that our identity is not wrapped up in our jobs, but in knowing that God has created us, and we are designed to give Him glory in all aspects of our lives, whether in good times, or in bad. So this is the story of our journey through unemployment and our opportunity to continue to rely on and trust God. We want to offer hope to those who face a similar journey and desire to give a glimpse into unemployment so others may find comfort on their journey as well. As I thought about writing a book about unemployment I asked God, "If this is what you want me to do I need you to help me as I put words to paper." At the beginning of September this year I woke up one morning and in a matter of a few minutes wrote down some chapter titles which I believe God gave me as the framework to build upon. Realizing that our hope is ultimately in a relationship with God I end each chapter with a prayer drawing our hearts and our thoughts to focus on Him.

The Day

*T*he new year of 2011 started off with a great milestone step as our son Joel, who graduated from college the year before with a music degree, was able to find a job working at a school in their music lab and studio. He also started serving part time as a worship leader in a church in Cambridge, Massachusetts. An even greater milestone was that he moved out of our home to an apartment near his job, to begin a life of total independence. Our daughter Jenna was continuing her undergraduate studies for a Social Work degree, and I was working part time as a registered nurse in a Boston hospital. Apart from some stress Mark was feeling at work from the "reorganization" seven months before, life was good.

As I imagined life after my kids were out of college, I did not see myself working but doing other things. I would envision spending more time volunteering, visiting the elderly, or leading a woman's Bible Study. I was even looking forward to going on several short term mission trips. The thought of total freedom and time to serve in these ways was appealing to me. My plan was to rely on Mark's salary, for after all he would be working for at least another 12 years, or so I thought. It is so interesting how we often forge ahead with plans in our life as if things are always going to go smoothly or as envisioned. In Proverbs 16:9 it says "In his heart a man plans his course, but the Lord determines his steps." (NIV) In the beginning of January 2011 the Lord was indeed "determining our steps" in a different direction.

A snowstorm was predicted for the evening of January 26, 2011, but I was determined to accomplish my laid out plans for the day. I had no idea that a storm of another kind was beginning to brew. I had the day off from work and had planned a variety of chores and errands. At 9 am I got out of the bank and was about to head to the gym when my cell phone rang. It was Mark wondering what I was doing that afternoon and asked if I would like to spend some time with him. In my mind he was sabotaging my plans, and I was feeling a little frustrated since I had things to do, but I readjusted my thinking and said I would be happy to spend some time with him. He then said, "Actually I think you will be spending a lot more time with me". I was confused and wondered what that meant. "I was just let go from my job and was told that my position was eliminated", he said plainly. I had an inner gasp, but also a sense of calm and peace, and all I could think to say was, "God is good, we know God is good." I remembered the words of a pastor of ours who would always say, "God is good...all the time!" I expressed how sorry I felt for him and my heart ached for the husband I loved.

As he began his day at work, he retold, he arrived at the usual time of 7:30 am to check his emails and plan the events of his day. Then a call came from his boss, with the words, "meet me in HR". As Mark proceeded to the Human Resource department he initially thought to himself that something bad was going to happen to someone, and then he immediately realized that "the something bad" was going to happen to him. When he realized this he began to pray and God gave him a peace and calm to be prepared for the news he was about to receive. The meeting in the Human Resource office was brief and the news was delivered directly and to the point by his boss, "your position has been eliminated", "we appreciate your efforts on behalf of this company", and "any questions?" His boss left and Mark remained to finish up talking about details with the HR Director.

Graciously he was offered the day to wrap things up in his office and have the opportunity to say some good-byes to people he had known and worked with for so long. Many people are not treated with this dignity when faced with the news of their job loss. Most are escorted by security guards to clean out their desks, and then walked to the door, carrying the leftovers from all their working life in a box never to return. When Mark came back to his office he was greeted by about 12 people who had worked for him and with him, for they heard the news from their new boss at the same time as he had. There were expressions of disbelief and words of support and sympathy for him.

After hearing this news my mind started spinning and my plans for the day were placed on hold. I called my closest friend and my brother, because I needed to tell someone, but I also knew that they would pray. I notified Joel and Jenna and asked if they would be available to meet Dad and me for dinner at one of our favorite restaurants because I thought it was important we be together as a family to support one another. Joel and Jenna and I arrived first at the restaurant, and shortly we spotted Mark in the parking lot. As he walked toward us I had the first flood of tears. I thought of him having to walk out of the front doors of the company he loved for the very last time that day and that image filled me with sadness. As we ate our meal that night I don't know that any of us really tasted our food, but the time was so rich and meaningful. As he shared the events of the day, Mark talked of how he felt, and how many people came by to say good-bye. During the day he sought out others to say how much he appreciated them. He had a few times of tears during the day and as he described one of those times Mark's eyes began to well up. A co-worker, Ken, who had been a prior fire chief in one of the local towns, stopped by Mark's office to give Mark a medallion he used to give to his firefighters who demonstrated "courage and valor". He wanted Mark to have it because of his respect for him. Mark was moved by this kind gesture.

To be supported by our children on this day was a beautiful experience. Our daughter, Jenna bought her father one of his favorite types of candies. I think she wanted to convey in a tangible way that her Dad was loved and special. She is such a sympathetic listener and "cheer giver" and there was comfort in her presence. After Mark had finished sharing about his day, Joel then spoke and said he wanted to tell us about his day. He began by saying he started a project at work which he felt had needed to be done for awhile. The project was cleaning up and organizing the music studio. As he began to tell us he choked up in tears and was unable to get the words out, and as we waited for what he had to say, he finally spoke in tears and sobs, "Dad, as I was cleaning up the music studio, I was thinking of you and how you had to clean out your office today, and what you must be feeling, and that you would not be returning." We were all in tears by that time. I think the waitress was a little baffled by the scene.

As Mark and I look back on the beginning of our unemployment journey, this is a day we would never take back and wish never happened. It was a memorable time as a family and in the midst of tears great joy was experienced because of God's support through that day, but also the love of our children. I know that each of you have your memories of your own "day", the day that began your unemployment journey. Remembering that day may bring back feelings of sadness, shock, and sometimes even resentment or anger. To go on from that day forward takes courage, fortitude, and a determination that this will not defeat you.

Prayer:

Dear Lord,

It is our prayer that we totally trust you. Help us not to rely on human strength but trust in your almighty hand to guide. Keep us from the temptation of just jumping in on our own to try to "fix" things, but give us patient hearts to wait on you. We ask also that you will be with others who have heard the news of their job loss, or those that will, and pray for a measure of strength and peace for them.

God's Provision

*T*he very real tangible needs that loom ahead of each person and family during a time of unemployment may be different. We knew for us that this was an opportunity to see how God would provide. In an ideal world, employers would take inventory of the personal life of their employees when planning to dismiss them. However, this would make a difficult task even harder as they thought of how the loss of this job may impact a person's life. It is a business decision, cut and dry, calculating and cool, and just a fact of life; you miss out, no more "available chairs" for you. In our case the ideal employer would ask the following: "Does Mark have family members with medical needs facing surgery and losing his job would mean loss of health insurance?" or "Does he still have to put a child through college?" "Is there anyone else in the family that works that may be able to provide to meet financial needs?" "Is he taking care of an elderly mother in his home that relies on him?" These were some of the needs and realities of life we were facing.

Throughout our life we have been thankful for God's gracious provision and have been blessed in so many ways. Now that we were faced with these particular needs we looked forward to how God would provide. In the Old Testament there are many different names for God which were used to show some aspect or characteristic of his nature, and one of these names is *Jehovah Jireh*, which means *God the Provider*. Knowing that we have trusted God with our life we were confident that God would indeed provide.

Our first challenge was to get medical insurance. To our surprise Mark's medical insurance was cut off at midnight the day of his dismissal. He was told that he could sign up for COBRA which is a provision for a dismissed employee to continue on the employer's health plan for a temporary period of time, but the ex-employee would be responsible for the full premium, and in our case that would be $2,000 per month. I guess we could be thankful that Mark didn't lose his job before 1985 because that was the year Congress enacted COBRA (Consolidated Omnibus Budget Reconciliation Act) which gave the provision for extending insurance coverage after job loss.[1] I do wonder how realistic it is for most people to afford $2,000 a month especially without a job! I think COBRA is so aptly named because it is like a cobra taking a lethal bite out of the finances of those unemployed. Thankfully since I worked 24 hours a week at the hospital, I had enough hours to be able to sign up for my hospital's health plan. I needed to declare that we had a "life event", a loss of job, and it was no problem signing up. I was thankful that my employer made it an easy transition and both my son facing surgery and I would be covered. My job also was a provision to help meet financial needs as I was able to pick up extra shifts at the hospital.

Another way our needs were met was a fair

severance offered to Mark after his 10 years of service to his company. This was a check delivered to our home for one lump sum, but it was stunning to see that 42% of the total went to taxes. To receive the severance Mark had to sign a "Release of Claims", and at least in our state he was also able to sign up for unemployment benefits as well. As little as unemployment is, every bit helps! One tip a friend of ours shared who had experienced dismissal from their company several years prior was to not go to the unemployment office in person, because that would feel too despairing, but to just call and sign up over the phone. One has to be patient to do this because you may find yourself on hold for long periods of time as Mark did.

When you are without a job, the pressing need is to find a job and we were thankful that his former employer did provide outplacement services through a company called ClearRock, to give help with formulating his resume, writing cover letters, and interviewing techniques. It is important to get guidance for the "job transition" process, and for job seeking. Michael Melcher, author of *"The Creative Lawyer: A Practical Guide to Authentic Professional Satisfaction"* states that "many well-educated professionals are unaware of how ineffective some of their job-search strategies are. Most job-seekers spend too much time on the Internet and not enough time networking with real people."[2] Mark was so thankful for this help and for his very encouraging job coach, who guided him, gave him tips, cheered him along, and stressed that he needed to network, network, and network!

When you lose your job you begin to look for ways to cut back on expenses and minimize monthly bills. The last provision came in a rather unusual way, when one day shortly after Mark lost his job I was home from work and just about ready to go grocery shopping when Mark called. He had been at a networking lunch meeting several towns from us so I was surprised at his call. He asked if I minded picking him up since he was watching our brand new 2 month old car being towed away. He had just been in a rather serious accident where someone ran a stop sign, spun his car 360 degrees and head on into an on-coming car. Thankfully no one was hurt, but our car was totaled and was beyond repair. With the insurance money we bought an older used car and paid by cash, with no car loan. Now we have one less car payment per month, thus eliminating one bill we would have had to pay. You may say, how can you say that a car accident was God's provision? Well, all I know is that this was an accident that could have harmed several people, but no one was injured, except for the car, and now our monthly expenses have decreased.

There may be many who read this chapter and say, well "when I lost my job I got nothing!" No severance, no health insurance, no job seeking help, nothing. In experiencing this unemployment journey I know that we have gained more empathy for those who go through job loss, and receive so little, and are struggling just to make ends meet. I like the instructions from Paul to Timothy in I Timothy 6:17-19 which says "Tell those rich in this world's wealth to quit being so full of themselves and so obsessed with money, which is here today and gone tomorrow. Tell them to go after God, who piles on all the riches we could ever manage-to do good, to be rich in helping others, to be extravagantly generous. If they do that, they'll build a treasury that will last, gaining life that is truly life." (*The Message*) We know that our material wealth is just fleeting and will fade away, but seeking after God, seeking for His riches, He will always provide the needs that we have as we seek Him. From Matthew 6:25-34 we are reminded how our Father cares and knows our needs. The birds of the air, the lilies of the field God cares for, "are you not more valuable than they?"(NIV) The reality is our hearts are anxious, we do worry about tomorrow, and meeting the needs of our families, but God challenges us to have faith to rest in His provision to meet those needs. Seek Him first and rest in His care.

Prayer:

Dear Lord,

We thank you for how you have provided for us in

the past, presently, and will provide in the days to come. Help those who are struggling because of job loss and financial distress. As we trust in you help us to truly know that you are Jehovah Jireh, the God who provides, but mostly help us to always seek you first.

The New Norm

As I think about the particular routine of our days these past almost three decades of marriage I realize that there was a certain pace and rhythm of our life, and there was comfort in routine. For all those years Mark would get up early, usually by 5:30 am and get ready for his day with a time of quiet and breakfast. Mark's mother has lived with us the past three years due to health problems, so before leaving for work at 7:00 am he would give her a hug along with her morning meds, and say "I love you Mom." I remember when we were first married and I headed out the door to go to work I would often sullenly say, "I have to go to work", but Mark would always encourage me to say "I get to go to work". My statement emphasized the *obliga-*

tion of work, while his conveyed the positive joy of the *opportunity* of work. He faced each day not with drudgery, but recognizing the joy and privilege of work. The daily routine of leaving for work and then returning became as predictable as the ebb and flow of the tide—constant and steady. With job loss that equilibrium of routine is jolted off balance.

The first morning after being dismissed from his job Mark got up early at 4:00 am to snow blow our driveway since the snow storm came to pass, and our driveway needed to be cleared before I left for my 12 hour shift at the hospital. Afterwards, he came in to the warmth of the house to have breakfast, and contemplate on the events of the day before. When faced with negative situations, we all have the choice of how to respond. We can choose sadness and withdrawal, perhaps anger or bitterness. Mark chose worship. He sat in our living room that morning and sang hymns. At this time of challenge he sang, "Great is the Faithfulness" as an affirmation of God's faithfulness.

Great is the faithfulness O God my Father,

There is no shadow of turning with Thee;

Thou changest not; Thy compassions they
fail not;

As Thou hast been Thou forever wilt be

Great is thy faithfulness!

Great is thy faithfulness!

Morning by morning new mercies I see;

All I have needed Thy hand hath provided,

Great is Thy faithfulness, Lord unto me.[1]

Those moments of worship that morning I know were a healing balm to Mark's soul, but also brought joy to God's heart. You may say I can't sing, well one thing Mark is not noted for is his singing voice, but he always sings with enthusiasm and heartfelt expression to God. God really only asks us to "make a joyful noise" as we praise Him.

As Mark faced the days ahead he settled into a new norm. After hearing of his job loss, people would often say, "Now you have all this time to do some things you really like, or to tackle some projects around the house." People perceive that a benefit of unemployment is having time to yourself, and a great amount of it. Some go as far as to view unemployment as being on a perpetual vacation. The reality is that searching for a job is really a full time job of its own. Thus, Mark's new routine still included getting up early and preparing for the day with quiet and breakfast, and giving his Mom her morning meds and hug.

He spends most of his day on job seeking endeavors, internet searches, applying for jobs, adapting his resume, writing cover letters, networking calls, emails, and sometimes going to networking meetings. In the later afternoons he often goes for a long walk through the woods near our home. Other afternoons he will tackle needed projects around the house. Since losing his job he has had to fix a few mechanical things that have broken, like replacing a sewage ejector pump...not a pleasant affair! The other big projects have been painting a few sides of the house, and replacing a large deck doing all the labor himself. Sometimes taking time to do these physical projects give a rest to the mind, and relief from the monotony of the day, and the job searching grind.

One of the things he is committed to is taking the weekend off from his job search. He just chooses to do something different. Your mind needs to rest from the constant messaging of "I've got to get a job", "I've got to get a job", and as Mark likes to say, "I've got to make the donuts." Helpful advice we would offer to those who find themselves without a job would be to establish a routine for your day. It can become too tempting to just be swallowed up in the vast well of time, and find that you lose sight of purpose for your day and then just give up. A friend from church, also named Mark, had been the Vice President of Human Resources of North America for a large company before losing his job and experiencing a three and a half year journey with unemployment. He told about the anguish of some of those days.

"There were many days in those 3.5 years that were incredibly difficult. I only felt safe sitting on my couch in our front room, watching TV or looking for jobs on the computer. It became my little haven. The hardest days were the days that there was nothing to do at all. I hated those days, they dragged on forever and it allowed time for your mind to wander, wonder and worry."

Another friend, Karen who had worked at a Christian school for 23 years, most recently as principal, lost her job because the school had to close for financial reasons. She has been looking for employment for over a year. She describes the difficulties of the drudgery of the new routine.

"I would fill out an application, and wait. Send out resumes, and wait. Call for information, and wait. The lack of time that I had while working was now an endless stretch of days without things that I "had" to do...

except job seek."

Normally my husband has maintained a positive attitude through this journey of unemployment, but there was one day this past summer after seven months out of work that he seemed particularly down. When we sat on our deck for dinner and I conveyed to him the events of my day at work, I then asked him about his day. He very rarely looks discouraged, but he looked quite dejected and said, "I don't like my days." These days of the "new norm" are hard, tedious, and most often it is a lot of activity with not much fruit. I felt deeply for him because I could see how hard he was working to get a job, and for so long. I told him, "Then why don't you just stop for awhile?" and then I asked him "What have you always wanted to do but haven't had the time?" He then said, "I would like to hike the John Muir Trail in California". I know that hiking has been a great joy in his life and I just wanted to give him permission to stop this endless job search, and I could just try to work more at the hospital.

When he was 19 years old he had walked 1,000 miles of the Pacific Crest Trail with a friend, and that journey was spectacular in many ways. It was on that trip that he read the New Testament and was confronted with the truth of Jesus and what he had come to do, and Mark began his journey as a believer in Jesus from that time on. It would have been nice to take the time to walk that trail but Mark felt he had at least some momentum in the job search so he didn't want to interrupt it yet. Thus his hiking plans for the John Muir Trail have been placed on hold for now.

When I returned home from work that first day after Mark lost his job I asked him how his first day was. He told me about his worship time in the morning, but also that he fixed the snow blower since it broke earlier in the day. He basically had to dismantle it and found the broken part, replaced the part and put it back together. I was so impressed, and said "Honey, just like Napoleon Dynamite you have skills! Maybe you can become a snow blower repairman!" We had to find the humor.

Prayer:

Dear Lord,

Along with the psalmist we pray to teach us to number our days that we may gain a heart of wisdom. We are thankful for each day and we pray that they are full with your purpose and direction. Help us to persevere when the days seem long and the job search seems endless.

Wisdom from Some Old Books

*Early on in our unemployment journey our pastor was doing a sermon series in Job. For many Job is a familiar story and you may sit back and yawn, "I have heard it all before". For others it may be a fresh story to their ears, and particularly relevant for those experiencing a period of challenge. Job was faced with a series of catastrophic events in his life, first losing all his resources for livelihood, his oxen, sheep, and camels, then his own children, and lastly his very health as he became afflicted with painful sores from his head to his feet. During that time our pastor, Bernie Powell, wrote an article in our church's newsletter titled "*Alternate Education*". He said, "Among God's most effective classrooms are trial and adversity. We learn the deepest lessons when our hearts have been ripped open." He goes on to say that:

"The story of Job in the Bible starts with a scene of peace and prosperity and it closes with even greater prosperity. In between were forty chapters of crushing adversity and senseless loss. When does Job learn the most about God? When does life come in to the clearest focus? Not in the days of ease. It's when Job's heart is broken and he's at his wit's end that he goes the deepest with God."[1]

I know that this has been true in my life that when I have faced the times of greatest challenge I have been drawn closer to God and have learned the most. Our friend Mark again expresses so well how the story of Job even helped him:

"What kept me going was Job's example in

the Bible. He had everything going well, his future looked bright. What could go wrong? You all know the story-he lost everything that he held dear. There is that great moment in his story where he is sitting in a heap of ashes, beaten down, humbled, suffering and almost broken. He was even scrapping his open sores with pieces of broken pottery. His wife also suffering comes to him and says, "Do you still hold fast your integrity? Curse God and die!" I could relate to Job, I was hurting, I was down, I was depressed, hope was slipping away but I refused to let go of that glimmer of hope that was in Christ. Job's response to his wife was "...shall we indeed accept good from God and not accept adversity?" As my hope for a job and to keep my home was slipping away, I grasped on to Job's words to his wife. I hung my hat on those words with all I had left. No, I was not sure how long I could hold on to them, and I was pretty down at times but I knew that

I could not live with myself if I violated that principle."[2]

During times of testing in our lives we often seek out people who can offer wisdom and direction, and can also lend a listening ear. Shortly after losing his job Mark sought out a couple we knew who have these qualities. Loring had been one of the founding elders at our church and had since retired along with his wife Jeanne to a beautiful house on Cape Cod right on the Atlantic Ocean. Mark traveled to the Cape to share his journey with this older and wiser couple. As he told of his experience, they listened to him attentively and gave him a book that their small group at church was reading called *The Crook in the Lot*, which deals with the "sovereignty and wisdom of God displayed in the afflictions of men". A well-known Scottish Presbyterian minister named Thomas Boston who lived from 1676-1732 wrote the book. He and his wife Katherine had ten children, but only four survived and through the years she was plagued with declining health. He wrote this book about the adversities in life and spoke from the depth of his own experience. Boston's book written so many years ago is based on the verse from Ecclesiastes 7:13-14: "Consider what God has done: Who can straighten what He has made crooked? When times are good, be happy; but when times are bad, consider: God has made the one as well as the other." (NIV) This book is a wealth of insight and teaching on the subject of hardships we may face in our life, and I hope to focus on three teachings that impacted me in considering our present circumstance.

The *Realization* that God is Sovereign

Sovereignty means having "supreme authority and power". Those who believe in God must come to the realization that He is lovingly in charge of all things. The premise in this book is that whatever crook there is in one's lot in life is of God's making, and He is the one that can and will straighten it. Boston writes,

"There is a certain train or course of events, by the providence of God, falling to every one of us during our life in this world and that is our lot. In that train or course of events, some things fall out cross to us and against the grain; and these make the crook in our lot. While we are here there are cross events and agreeable ones in our lot and condition. Sometimes things are softly and agreeably gliding on; but by-and-by, there is some incident which alters that course, grates us, and pains us..."[3]

The starting point of resting our trust fully in God is to understand that He is solely in charge of all that touches our lives. The day of January 26th was no surprise to God and indeed this job loss has been allowed by God. It is hard for us to see for what purpose, but one thing we know, this has been an amazing growing and learning experience, one we would never have known if this did not happen. We have come to learn that, as Boston expresses it, "discerning your Father's hand in the crook will take out much of the bitterness of it, and will sugar the pill to you. For this cause it will be necessary to solemnly take God for your God under your crook. And in all your encounters with it, resolutely believe and claim your interest in Him."[4]

Our *Response* to the "crook in the lot"

We are perpetually faced with the choice of how we are going to respond to our crook or cross in life. Boston describes that sometimes we need to see that our response may be for the purpose of "giving rise to faith, hope, love, self-denial, resignation, and other graces, to many heavenly breathings, panting, and groaning, which otherwise would not be brought forth."[5] In Romans 5:3-4 we read that "we rejoice in our sufferings because we know that suffering produces perseverance; perseverance, character; and character, hope". (NIV) We realize that we are refined by the trials that come to us, and if we fully trust and rest in Him, the true fruit of "faith, hope, love, self-denial, resignation" can develop our character.

A mistake that too many people make in responding to their challenges is by focusing too much on the situation. Boston describes that there's "unsightliness" of each of our crooks, and notes, "Crooked things are unpleasant to the eye, and no crook in the lot seems to be joyous, but grievous. Therefore, men need to beware of giving way to their thoughts to dwell on their crook in the lot, and of keeping it too much in view."[6] In this way, the condition of unemployment is ever present on our minds. On our week vacation this summer, our relaxation and enjoyment was overshadowed by the thought, "Mark doesn't have a job, Mark needs a job". I would urge anyone in this situation to avoid the consuming effects of unemployment at all costs, and steer clear of unproductive fretting that will drain you of all your energy.

Another common response, Boston notes, is to fight against the "crook in the lot", and use all human effort to be freed from it:

"What makes the yoke gall our necks but that we struggle so much against it, and cannot let it sit at ease on us. How often are we in that case like men dashing their heads against a rock to remove it! The rock stands unmoved, but they are wounded and lose exceedingly by their struggle. Impatience under the crook lays an overweight on the burden and makes it heavier, while it weakens us and makes us less able to bear it."[7]

My daughter has steadfastly reminded me time and again, "Mom, you just have to trust God." The paradox of unemployment seems to be that the more effort that is put into relieving our situation, the harder it becomes. When we take matters into our own hands, we lose perspective that some things are out of our control. Indeed, we must be patient in order to see the fullness of God's provision.

"As to the crook in your lot, God has made it; and it must continue while He will have it so.

Should you apply your utmost force to even it or make it straight, your attempt will be vain; it will not alter it in spite of all that you can do. Only He who made it can mend it or make it straight."[8]

The story of our friend Mark's journey through unemployment has a happy ending and is a great example of how God works in His own time. Now employed at a start-up company Mark recalls, "All of my efforts to find a job produced nothing. He placed a job right at my feet! It was God's job, done God's way!"

Rightly Managing the Crook in Our Lot

Thomas Boston gives three directives for rightly managing what he calls the "application for removing the crook in our lot". He wisely instructs us to:

1. **Pray for it.**

   Matthew 21:22 "If you believe, you will receive

whatever you ask for in prayer."

Seek God in prayer, desire Him first, and praise Him at every opportunity you find. God wants us to ask for our needs, but He also just wants us to seek Him and be with Him.

2. **Humble yourself under its yoke**.

    I Peter 5:6 "Humble yourselves, therefore, under God's mighty hand, that he may lift you up in due time."

    Resist the desire to fight and fix things. Rest in God and know that He can provide. Find peace in this.

3. **Wait patiently till the Hand that made it mends it.**

    Isaiah 49:23..."those who hope in God will not be disappointed."

    Leave the timing of the deliverance to God and wait for Him to bring together the right job situation for you.[9]

As you apply these to your situation God will show how he is faithful.

Prayer:

Dear Lord,

I accept that this present "crook in my lot" is the work of your Hand and I know that you desire our good. Help me to humble myself under your hand and allow you to carry the weight of the burden instead of having me bucking and striving against you. Help me to be patient to wait on you and to see how you will straighten "the crook".

The Roller Coaster

*O*ne of my least favorite rides at the amusement park is the roller coaster. I just don't like the speed, the anticipation of the next curve or drop. It is a nail biting experience for me. The greatest elation I felt after the 82 second, 60mph spin on Aerosmith's Rockin' Roller Coaster at Disney was when it was over! I enjoy an adventure as do most people, but I am more of a merry-go-round type person; give me the steady, the known. I am not fond of the ups and downs of the roller coaster. The lyrics to a song my son wrote called *Carousel* talk about being drawn back to the simplicity of the tried and true carousel.

> I feel the sound of carousel music on the ground
> It runs up the legs of the ever changing crowd

These people look for the next ride of their lives
and base it on how they feel at that time

Lovers ride the Ferris wheel while daredevils try
To ride the fastest roller coaster
Before night's end, all turn to that faithful friend
And ride the old carousel

When I was young that carousel was where I would run
The wooden steed would call my name
But as I grew, I ignored its call for something new
I craved a stomach churning speed

On the drops of life's coasters I cannot
hold on tight enough to keep me sane
I want to be off those slick pleasure machines
And just ride that old carousel

I don't know why that carousel gives me hope
It's simple it never changes
Sitting on this roller coaster
I close my eyes and rewind the years

Chorus:

Round and round it goes

Smiles of clowns is all that it knows

Joy to all who ride

Unchanged it still satisfies[1]

Joel Schofield

To be sure, unemployment is an emotional roller coaster ride that will leave you drained physically and emotionally. The ups and downs of prospective job opportunities and great interviews, followed shortly after by a rejection letter or email leave you weak and weary. A recent study at Rutgers University found that those unemployed "experience anxiety, helplessness, and depression, stress and sleeping problems after losing their jobs."[2] On the Holmes and Rahe Stress Scale which rates events in an individual's life that produce stress, job loss rates 47 points out of 100. A discouraging figure for certain, but one that is sharply placed in perspective next to the death of a spouse at 100 points and divorce at 73 points.[3] Nonetheless, the many waves of emotions from joblessness are varied and far-reaching, ranging from struggles with self-esteem, sadness, frustration, and even loneliness. The accumulation of these feelings has been best described by my husband as a "gnawing feeling in the pit of your stomach".

Our first rise on the roller coaster began shortly after losing his job. Mark has often contemplated changing careers and for several years felt that God was laying a desire on his heart for full time ministry at the local church. Though this career change would nearly halve his prior paycheck, he was excited about serving and ministering in this way. Over twenty years Mark has been involved in our own church as an elder and volunteer, and puts in an average of 10-20 hours a week into various responsibilities including the finance team, facilities team, and sound and technology. He is the quintessential "go to person" for many issues at the church. His leadership has been valued, for example when he championed a 3 million dollar project building a new worship center in the past several years. Through these experiences, his thoughts turned towards the possibility of transitioning into a role as a full time church administrator.

A few weeks after Mark lost his job there was a posting on an internet job site for "Church Administrator" for a very large church in Boston. New England is not known for large churches, so this appeared to be a rare opportunity. We thought "Wow, this is it...taken out of one job and then God immediately provides!" He applied for the job and was contacted for an interview. There was a sense of anticipation, excitement, and even awe at how this was being put together. Our emotions were at a peak. The interview was very preliminary but turned out to be quite awkward and dysfunctional, and he went away feeling "wowed" in a different sense, and felt the impact of the roller coaster for the first time. A week passed and he got the first rejection, "Thank you, but we are pursuing other candidates that better match our needs." We felt confused and wondered how to reconcile Mark's sense of calling to this type of ministry with not getting this job.

Several months went by and Mark began dealing with another church which also had this need of administrative help. As the discussion with the pastor and church leadership began, a sense of enthusiasm built considering the possibility that God would use him to help support ministry as an administrator. The leadership met one week and had consensus to move forward with considering Mark for this type of position. With the next week came another meeting where the decision was reversed and they concluded, "No, this is not the direction we should go." Hearing this news Mark felt crushed. This was a different type of feeling than when he lost his job. He said that in losing his job there was grief over the loss, but mostly over the loss of relationships he had developed through the years. This current rejection was puzzling for him, and then he began to wonder if perhaps God wanted him in another situation. With two rejections for his church administrator dreams passed, Mark continued onward.

On this job search roller coaster ride there are

different types of rejections but I think the most difficult type is being "Franked". This is a phrase that came into our family after an experience our son Joel had as he entered his last year of college. For a long time Joel has liked music and is gifted in writing and composing songs, producing and writing his first CD in high school. He pursued his passion for music in college, graduating with a music degree. On his way back to school for his senior year he stopped in New York to meet with a music producer, and tour the studio and was introduced to a few of the people working there. This producer was named Frank (not his real name). As they met together Joel had a great discussion with him, even to the point of Frank telling Joel that he wanted him to "come and work for me after you graduate", "look me up", and "send me the music you write and I will listen to it." The offer was discussed in detail, and Joel came out of that meeting elated and walking on a cloud. This opportunity seemed to fall right into his lap; it was too good to be true. Indeed, as the year progressed Joel discovered that it was "too good to be true."

All attempts at communicating with Frank, via email, phone, and even snail mail failed. He never answered or acknowledged, and never responded to Joel at all. Needless to say Joel graduated with his music degree, but is *not* working for Frank. Joel learned the valuable lesson that people will often promise the "world" to you but not follow through. Joel found truth in the old saying, "you're only as good as your word" and discovered the importance of character and integrity. On Mark's journey, we have found that there have been many times when Mark would have a great networking meeting or interview and there would be enthusiasm and promises in the interaction, followed by no news, and no follow-up, just communication shut down. These are the rejections we like to call being "Franked", and they are particularly hard to take because we feel let down by the lack of integrity and broken promises.

The ups and downs of Mark's job search over this past year continued on in this way. There would be a call to come in to a company where he interviewed with 5 different people all in one day and then he'd hear nothing for over a month, only to learn that they decided "not to fill the position". The jobs that Mark would apply to would fall far short of the meaningful job he was dismissed from, and he struggled to find an opportunity with a worthwhile mission. Great prospects that would at first seem interesting and challenging would ultimately turn out to be a little hollow. The roller coaster took a swing upward after an amazing interview and meeting with a senior level executive for a company. Mark felt confident in the movement towards a job offer, until the roller coaster swung downward upon hearing the news that the position had lost its funding. The cycle of anticipation and rejection has been difficult to handle. After awhile you begin to face the anticipatory rise of the roller coaster with each new potential opportunity or interview with a sense of numbness and reserve, and with a guarded heart. This constant cycle of the up and down can leave your emotional nerve endings raw.

All of us in unemployment have these experiences; it is the universal challenge of job searching. A friend of Mark's who he meets together with periodically to discuss progress on their job searching endeavors had a similar hard rejection. He had flown out for two interviews, and the last interview was so positive, that he was told "I really like you and feel you are the best candidate" and was apparently one of the last two to be considered for the job. Yet, the company chose the other candidate. Rejection! A punch in the gut! But you move on. Recently Mark experienced a three month process for the possibility to become general manager of an engineering firm with four interviews during that time period with considerable travel back and forth for each interview. He really liked the company and those in leadership, and had amazing interviews and interactions. He was never quite sure whether they were just pursuing him or were there other candidates as well. After the Christmas holidays and this three month process Mark got the email that said, "We regret to inform you that we offered the position to another candidate who accepted", however Mark was "runner-up" for the position. "Runner-up" doesn't get you the job!

At the beginning of the week when I was writing this chapter I felt particularly frustrated because there just seemed to be no prospects or leads to pursue for that week. By the end of the week, however Mark had four phone interviews, many of them promising. So at the beginning of the week you feel low and in the trough of the roller coaster and then by the end of the week you are on the anticipatory rise. Reflecting on how God has directed his days, Mark will say, "Let's just take one day at a time." All I can say is that I am sticking with the carousel, which gives "joy to all who ride, unchanged it still satisfies."

Prayer:

Dear Lord,

We ask for your strength during the ups and downs of emotions that we have felt in the journey of a job search. Help us to hold on to the fact that you never change and you are always faithful and we trust in You, for you are a loving kind Father who desires good for his children. May our prayer be that expressed in I Peter 5:10 "...that after we have suffered a little while, restore us and make us strong, firm and steadfast."

The Scarlett "U"

*D*uring the journey through unemployment the sense of being an outcast is not uncommon. At the very beginning Mark was told by his job coach to always say that he was in "job transition". He was not to use statements like, "I am out of work", "I am unemployed", or "I was let go from my job". There is no doubt that this sugarcoated phrase sounds more positive, but it doesn't reflect the whole truth. In some ways, it sounds like the choice is voluntary, that one is just looking for new opportunities. When Mark has told someone he was in "job transition", some people have said, "Oh that's nice!" That's nice? Do they really know what they are saying? The fact is you are out of a job, you are unemployed, and this is an uncomfortable position to be in.

While visiting friends in California I read an article in the Fresno Bee newspaper titled, *Is U.S. Losing Patience with Jobless?* The author of the article, Tony Pugh stated a few shocking realities about those who find themselves unemployed. He writes, "many jobless American's say they sense a growing indifference to their plight, and even a certain level of demonization." A pretty harsh statement for sure, but the more days, and weeks you are unemployment this stigma does feel more of a reality. He goes on to write:

> *"For years, people who lost their jobs were the sad, sympathetic faces of the nation's economic meltdown. But more than two years after the Great Recession officially ended, America's empathy for the unemployed is showing signs of wear...Many companies now shun the long term unemployed when filling positions, fearing their skills have eroded or their talents don't measure up"*[1]

After reading that article I wrote in my journal that "this just seems like another daunting obstacle as we look at it, the stigma of the unemployed, the Scarlet "U" emblazoned on the chest, 'Unemployed'." Like Hester Prynne from *The Scarlet Letter*, those who are unemployed sometimes feel the same scorn and carry a badge of shame upon them. It's difficult for those on the outside to realize the strong desire from the 14 million unemployed to find a job and the frustration of not being able to get your foot in the door. It begins to seem as though the hundreds of resumes that are sent out enter into a black hole, never to be seen again.

On the other side of that black hole, companies that are hiring become overwhelmed and are inundated with thousands of applications. A local town near us received 250 applications for a clerk's job at the town hall, and noted that in the past they may have only gotten 4 or 5 applications for a job like this. A few months past and there was even an article in the newspaper about the lucky woman who did get the job, with her picture and all. You would think she had won the lottery. In some sense she did.

As time goes on in your unemployment journey it feels even more overwhelming to find a job. You feel like the deck is stacked against you. Rich Lowry, editor of the National Review writes:

> *"According to the Wall Street Journal, nearly a third of the unemployed, 4 million people have been out of work for more than a year. Almost half of the unemployed have been out of a job for more than six months, a figure higher than during the Great Depression. He goes on to say that "the insidious thing about long-term unemployment is that it builds on itself, the longer you are without a job the harder it is to get one. The Bureau of Labor Statistics finds that the chance of someone unemployed for less than five weeks finding a job in the next month is about 30 percent. For someone unemployed 27 weeks or more, it's just 10 percent."[2]*

There are 13 people who are unemployed on our prayer list at church, which is the most we have had in the last several years. Many people on this list have been out of work for over a year. When you are the one unemployed, it almost feels like some sort of epidemic. Yet to those with jobs, the condition of widespread unemployment seems only like a sad statistic. In the last several months I have had many conversations with people who have experienced job loss, and all their stories have the similar thread of humiliation and unfairness. They too experienced feelings of isolation and a sense of feeling shunned in the months that followed.

It is exceedingly difficult for the person who is older to find employment, regardless of their vast experience. Most companies are not willing to invest in bringing someone on who is older, who may only have 5-10 more years to work. I have talked to so many who have lost their jobs at 50 or 60 and it is so sad to hear their stories of how hard it has been for them to gain employment. One man was dismissed from his company after 32 years of employment at age 60 just before he was to donate his kidney to his ailing son, and now at age 62 is still trying to find another job. Recently I spoke to a woman who told me her husband was dismissed from his job at age 49 and was told he was "obsolete". She said with a sense of sadness, "Can you imagine being told you are obsolete at age 49?" Those who are older seeking employment appear to have another "U" imprinted on their chest, "Untouchables". While many companies could benefit from their years of experience and wisdom, there is little opportunity for these "older workers". The anguish cry of the unemployed is expressed by the actor Chris Cooper in *Company Men* when he says "Nothing changed. The newspaper comes every morning. The automatic sprinkler shuts off at 6 am", and then says "My life ended...Nobody noticed."[3] That is often the feeling many express in their unemployment; "Does anybody notice?" It can be a lonely journey.

In times of isolation and rejection, I am reminded of Psalm 32:7 "You are my hiding place; you will protect me from trouble and surround me with songs of deliverance." (NIV) God is ever present, ever caring, and a place of rest and solace when faced with the sense of desperation and loneliness on this unemployment journey.

Prayer:

Dear Lord,

During the times of loneliness and isolation help us to realize that you are our "hiding place", a shelter from the storm. And in those times when we feel or sense the scorn of the world as to what our value is, remind us of what you have said how we are valued. Thank you for your words expressed in Jeremiah 29:11 as to how much you care for us, "For I know the plans I have for you declares the Lord, plans to prosper you and not to harm you, plans to give you hope and a future." (NIV)

Merry Heart Moments

While driving on the highway, Mark and I saw a bumper sticker on a truck that caught our attention. It said "Do not postpone joy!" We both resonated with this thought and realized the importance of not "postponing joy" in the midst of our struggles. I recently read a delightful book called *The Hedge People* by Louise Carey, in which she describes her experiences taking care of her 92-year-old father-in-law who had Alzheimer's. Her stories are fun and sad, charming and poignant. One of the phrases from the book that I have latched onto in our present circumstance is, "If you smile at life, life will smile back at you."[1] She also speaks of what she calls "merry heart moments", noting that Proverbs 17:22 states a "cheerful (merry) heart is good medicine, but a crushed spirit dries up the bones." (NIV) After reading her book, I realized the importance of taking the time to smile and find the joy in each day.

On this journey we have experienced some "merry heart moments" of our own. Early on when we were feeling particularly dejected and sad, I was cleaning out my son's room and came across a bumper sticker that said *igbok*: "it's going to be o.k." My son got this bumper sticker from the church he attended during college when they were doing a series on I Thessalonians "His Coming-Our Hope". The *igbok* website describes the idea for this saying:

"What if God, the creator, sustainer and redeemer of creation made this promise? What if He shouted and whispered "igbok" from Genesis to Revelation? He's the only one who could make this promise-and keep it. If He did, then we have reason to hope...We think He did. God's "o.k." doesn't mean that the cancer will be healed, the relationship

fully restored, the physical pain or emotional ache will go away in this life. It means that because He has entered and overcome our brokenness...we can live this life with real hope-a hope that knows one day everything will be set right forever in the life to come."[2]

That sticker is posted on our mirror as a daily reminder that because of our hope in God "it's going to be O.K." Some merry heart moments, come to you like that bumper sticker.

Other's come more subtly, during long walks or bike rides or day trips to Cape Cod. Mark has a few of his own during a three day hike with our daughter into the White Mountains of New Hampshire. Beside the beauty of the mountains, the physical exertion of the hike carrying the heavy backpacks, sleeping in a hut, the joy of being with Jenna was unsurpassed. Another time we brought a picnic dinner to Lexington, MA and met our son Joel, and walked in the Minute Man National Park.

When making life adjustments in unemployment, it is important not to strip yourself of the things that bring fun and joy. Early on after losing his job Mark thought perhaps he should sell our ski boat so I wouldn't have the anxiety about our financial state. When I found out he was planning to sell the boat I told him not to because I knew what a wonderful joy and outlet waterskiing has been for him. I said, "You just lost your job, you can't lose that too." Perhaps some time in the future we'll have to sell the boat, but it's important to me to hold onto it if we can.

Hike with Jenna

Mark Enjoying Skiing

About seven months in to Mark's unemployment journey, our daughter was visiting at her boyfriend's house and began talking with his father about how difficult it can be when people lose their jobs. Jenna expressed to him how she felt her father was not treated fairly in the circumstances of being let go from his job. When she named the company where Mark had worked, he remarked that his former college roommate and good friend worked there as Vice President. When he said his friend's name, Jenna turned white in shock. Her boyfriend's father asked, "That wasn't the person who let your father go, was it?" Sure enough it was. God knew all along of this connection, and revealed it at just the right time to give us a little smile. Merry heart moment! Who doesn't think that God has a sense of humor? The connection was uncanny.

Our family has had some fun lately with fortune cookies at Chinese restaurants. Here are a few:

"An unexpected relationship will become permanent."

"Sometimes traveling to a new place leads to great transformation."

"You will soon create a favorable impression on someone."

But our all time favorite is:

"You will be called to fill a position of high honor and responsibility."

And the most recent:

"Do you believe? Endurance and persistence will be rewarded."

Some of the greatest merry heart moments have been through the encouragement and love of family and friends. There are genuine expressions of concern and constant reminders that others are praying for us. Most recently we had a fun spontaneous moment as Mark's Harley riding doctor rode to our house on an unusually warm January day, and knocked on our door. We shared together around our kitchen table; he listened, he prayed, and then rode off. With these merry heart moments we are reminded, "God is good".

Prayer:

Dear Lord,

You have said "Rejoice in the Lord Always" and "The joy of the Lord is our strength". Help us to treasure the joyful moments on our journey, the merry heart moments, but mostly help us to first seek you as the giver of true joy.

Ten Truths for the Journey

As we have passed through these many months of unemployment I have come across statements or teachings in my devotional readings, many from *My Utmost for His Highest* by Oswald Chambers that have been "truth points" for me. These have served as mile markers as a take on each new day and are overall principles to face the challenges of unemployment, or for any challenges in our life.

1. Don't look at your circumstances...look beyond.

There is a story in Matthew 14 where in the midst of a storm Jesus walks on water toward the boat his disciple's were sailing. When they saw Jesus they were terrified, but he reassured them, "Take courage. It is I, don't be afraid." Impulsively, Peter immediately asks to walk to Jesus on the water. As he proceeds toward Jesus, he is frightened by the wind and waves and begins to sink. Jesus quickly reached out his hand to Peter to save him, but while doing so asks, "You of little faith, why did you doubt?"

There are times in our unemployment journey that we only keep looking at our circumstances. "The things around you are real (circumstances), but when you look only at them you are immediately overwhelmed, and even unable to recognize Jesus."[1]

2. "I am with you to deliver you." (Jeremiah 1:8)

"If life or circumstances seem unfair or unjust let God be the one to deliver you. Never look for justice in this world, but never cease to give it."[2] There was a point in our journey when both Mark and I had to let go of our feelings

78

that he had been treated unfairly in the circumstances of his dismissal, and the feeling that it just didn't make sense. There have been times when I have driven by his old company on my way somewhere else, and was filled with feelings of great sadness and resentment. This thinking is not helpful, and we had to release the feelings of desiring justice in this situation. There has been a freedom since letting go and accepting fully that God is the righteous and fair judge who does deliver in His appointed time. It is important not to hold on to anger, as I Corinthians 13:5 says that love "...is not easily angered, it keeps no record of wrongs."(NIV) Release yourself from these negative feelings in order to move on and heal. I like how Eugene Peterson expresses this principle in *The Message* in Psalm 37 "Bridle your anger, trash your wrath, cool your pipes-it only makes things worse."(The Message)

3. "Do not fret for it only causes harm"

The effects of stress can have a negative impact on your physical and emotional health, and more importantly your soul. "Have you been propping up your soul with the idea that your circumstances are too much for God to handle?"[3] You must rest in God.

4. Resist the temptation of retreating when you're being tested in your unemployment journey.

There have been times when I have felt like hibernating and being withdrawn from others. I have found it to be beneficial to spend time with friends and family in order to share about our journey but not dwell on it. Right after hearing of Mark's job loss a couple in our neighborhood who have become our close friends invited us over for pot roast and potato and gravy dinner. That was the best meal shared with friends during a hard time. Steve McVey in his book

Walking in the Will of God states that "life's circumstances can sometimes come at you with such violence and force that you are tempted to hunker down".[4] Resist the temptation to hide and isolate.

5. **Keep your mind filled with the concept of God's control over everything.**

Matthew 7:11 "...how much more will your Father who is in heaven give good things to those who ask Him."(NIV)

"At times God may appear as an unkind friend, but He is not, He may appear like an unnatural father but He is not. He may appear like an unjust judge, but He is not...Not even the smallest detail of life happens unless God's will is behind it."[5] During this time of unemployment I have often felt like God is silent. In my prayers, in my earnestly seeking Him, I have not heard a clear answer, or clear direction as to what path to go. This has been hard to experience, and is best expressed in a devotional sent to me by a friend several years ago titled *Discipline's of Life* by Raymond Edman. "The darkness brings to us haunting shadows that insinuate, "God has forgotten to be gracious." But we should "never doubt in the dark what God told you in the light."[6] We must continue to trust in God even in the dark moments of our lives. The words of an old hymn reinforce this truth.

O for a faith that will not shrink,

Tho' pressed by every foe,

That will not tremble on the blink

Of any earthly woe!

That will not murmur nor complain

Beneath the chastening rod,

But, in the hour of grief or pain,

Will lean upon its God;

A faith that shines more bright and clear

When tempests rage without

That when in danger knows no fear,

In darkness feels no doubt.[7]

–William H. Bathurst

6. Depend on God's Presence.

"Our problems arise when we refuse to place our trust in the reality of His presence."[8] Can you imagine how different each day would be if we acknowledged God's presence in each moment of the day and hold on to the fact that he is "ever present" with you?

7. What is my vision of God's purpose for me?

"Whatever it may be, His purpose is for me to depend on Him and on His power now." "His purpose is the process itself. It is the process, not the outcome that is glorifying to God."[9] How am I bringing glory to God in this process of being unemployed? We always look for the outcome, or always look for what tomorrow will bring instead of living in the moment now. What is

God's will today?

8. The teaching of adversity

"In the world you will have tribulation. The strain of life is what builds our strength. God never gives us strength for tomorrow, or for the next hour, but only for the strain of the moment."[10]

9. "Be living trophies of God's grace"[11]

Apart from just liking the sound of that phrase I think this holds a truth on how our response to our situation of unemployment can reflect to other's God's grace. Are we constantly complaining or bemoaning our circumstance or does our calm trust in God shine forth in our countenance, or even in our interactions with others.

10. "Produce complete and utter joy in the heart of Jesus by remaining absolutely confident in Him, in spite of what we are facing."[12]

The thought of bringing "joy in the heart of Jesus" is something I had never pondered before, and I desire even more to bring him joy as we totally trust him for the next opportunity for Mark.

Prayer:

Dear Lord,

Help us to keep some of these truths in our minds as we go about our days. Help us to realize that you care about our journeys and that you desire to even build our character in the midst of our current situations. In everything we desire to bring you glory and praise.

If I Ran the Zoo

*T*hrough this process of unemployment both Mark and I have contemplated about the way of doing business and how even though we realize there are harsh realities and tough decisions companies have to make, we would like to think there is a better way. One of my favorite children's books is *If I Ran the Zoo* by Dr. Seuss. It begins, "...if I ran the zoo," said young Gerald McGrew, "I'd make a few changes. That's just what I'd do..."[1] I have often thought about that in various situations in life, that if we had the opportunity how would we run or handle things differently.

One way is basing your business practices on **ethical standards**. I like the interaction in the movie *Company Men* in the scene where the character played by Tommy Lee Jones is in a meeting to discuss who was going to be dismissed next. At one point in that meeting he says, "What about ethical scrutiny?" When he was assured by his co-worker that, "We are not breaking any laws." Jones replies "I guess I always assumed we were trying for a higher standard than that."[2] There is a yearning that companies would seek to act honorably and compassionately instead of being ruled by the all mighty dollar. I like the stories of two companies whose owners acted with a high level of integrity even though they both faced potential financial disasters due to fires.

The first example is Aaron Feuerstein, the third-generation owner and CEO of Malden Mills in Lawrence, Massachusetts. On December 11, 1995 this factory burnt down. He chose to use the insurance money not only to rebuild, but also spent millions to keep all 3,000 of his employees on the payroll for 6 months with full benefits. He based his decision on his religious conviction and the teaching of the *Talmud* as he said,

"I have a responsibility to the worker, both blue-collar and white-collar. I have an equal responsibility to the community. It would have been unconscionable to put 3,000 people on the streets and deliver a death-blow to the cities of Lawrence and Methuen. Maybe on paper our company is worthless to Wall Street, but I can tell you it is worth more."[3]

Because of his loyalty and commitment to his employees, he was awarded the Peace Abbey Courage of Conscience Award on March 13, 1998. People could argue that because of his actions he eventually lost the company to bankruptcy so it may have not been a wise move, the point is he cared deeply about his employees and his religious convictions that called him to a higher standard.

Another example is a company I read about in our local newspaper, *The Enterprise* on September 28, 2011 in an article written by Charles Kelleher Harris. "Just after 10 o'clock one Saturday night in 2008, Bill

Nixon watched his dream go up in smoke. An electrical mishap was to blame for the blaze that swept through Nixon's company, Willwork Inc. of Easton. At the time of the fire, Willwork Inc. employed 60 people, most of them local residents. The day after the fire, all 60 employees showed up at the site to begin cleanup. A new location nearby was set up as a temporary office and by that Monday, Willwork Inc. was up and running."[4]

I find it remarkable the dedication of those 60 workers to respond on a Sunday to help save their company. Just recently renovations have been completed and they have moved back in to their original site. This company has grown to a national business with 15 locations across the country and in just last year the company grossed $14 million. In the article Nixon, the 82 year old owner of the company states that, "Ninety-five percent of our employees are local." "We want to see the locals do well." It is in hiring people who are local the company got its name. "It is called Willwork because it creates work," said Director of Business Management Bob

McGlincy.[5] Not only do they hire local; they support other local businesses by using their services as well. This just seems like an amazing model for companies to follow, and in doing so benefit from the solid commitment and loyalty of their employees.

Secondly, "if we ran the zoo" we would focus on **simplicity**. In the book *Search of Excellence* by Thomas Peters and Robert Waterman we read, "The excellent companies were, above all, brilliant on the basics. Tools did not substitute for thinking. Intellect didn't overpower wisdom. Analysis didn't impede action. Rather, these companies worked hard to keep things simple in a complex world."[6] With the current trend to follow "complex organizational development" models, many companies are jumping on the bandwagon. Now certainly organization and order are good, and it is important for companies to evaluate their practices and how they could improve, but sometimes this creates havoc with the people who actually work in these companies. Because things have become more regimented and defined, often the employee doesn't find their work as meaningful, or that they are as valued.

I spoke with a woman who works at a large insurance company we do business with, who was just about to retire after over 30 years of employment. I said to her that I was always impressed with how efficient people were when we had to deal with any insurance matters, and that we were very pleased with our interactions with this company. She said that it has been a great company to work for, but she also described a time a few years ago when the organizational experts came in to improve things, and all it seemed to do was decrease employee's morale. Thus the company decided to go back to the prior policies.

Mark's elimination of his job centered on an organizational restructuring and was championed by the "organizational development specialists". Theoretically organizational development seems fine but sometimes its implementation in the real world is very complex and treats people more like pawns to be shuffled around. Mark interviewed for a job at a large company, which seemed like it would be a good match with his skills and background in training. One thing the interviewer kept asking and stressing is "Did he have experience with EVM (Earned Value Management)?" Mark has described this EVM as "project management on steroids". Again this perked my curiosity and began to learn a little more about it and discovered that it is a rather complex approach to project management with a multiplicity of formula's, calculations and graphs. I thought to myself I could not imagine how any company could get anything done being bogged down in its' complexity. So I guess the bottom line for us is to keep things simple with clear policies and goals and treat your employees as one of your greatest assets.

Lastly you should not underestimate the value of **leadership.** I used to kid Mark that he seemed to have the knack of Tom Sawyer who was able to get several of the young boys in town to whitewash Aunt Polly's fence and have them want to do it. Somehow Mark has been able to organize people for a project and get them excited about doing it. Many a time I would find the rake in my hand after he encouraged me to come out and "enjoy the fresh air", and then I would see him at another corner of the yard starting a different project. He has always liked working building teams to accomplish a common goal and try to work to people's strengths. When breaking up a team as happened at his company they lost the sense of synergy and each member of the team was now put in a position of working more in isolation, instead of drawing on the strengths of each other, or being guided by a leader with vision. Through the years I have also seen that Mark is a creative thinker, many times coming up with "out of the box" solutions to problems.   As we contemplate opportunities for Mark in the future our desire would be that he could work at a place that values ethical standards, and integrity; one that is not so entwined with the complexity of organizational matrix's and procedures which tend to dampen the creativity and full use of a person's talents; and lastly one where true leadership is recognized to provide the vision and compass for others to follow.

Prayer:

Dear Lord,

We pray that we would be people of integrity who treat one another with respect and honor. As we are in the process of seeking a new job, lead us to those who also value ethical standards, a simplicity but willingness to have freedom and ingenuity, and also those that value the gift of leadership. Be our constant guiding light.

A Wife's Reflections

As a wife I often think of how I may support my husband during this time. For the most part, this year has been about how we have been propping each other up. Sometimes Mark needs encouragement and I can come alongside to be there for him, but other times it is I who needs the encouragement. When we first started this journey I wrote down questions to ask Mark as we sat for dinner one evening. I offer them as a guideline for discussion as others may face the same journey of unemployment:

1. How are you feeling? What are your emotions?
2. If you do have any negative emotions what are they centered on? The reason?

3. Do you feel God directing or guiding you in any particular way?

4. You are always optimistic. Do you feel optimistic? Why? Or Why not?

5. What do YOU want to do? What do you like, what do you envision yourself doing?

6. Help me think through the finances. What is it we need to meet our financial obligations?

7. Are there practical things I can do to help support you during this time?

In this past year my heart has ached for the husband I love. Through three decades of marriage, Mark and I have grown in our understanding of the words of Genesis 2:24, when "two shall become one" as a husband and wife. Through the many experiences of these past years, which have been full of joy and encouragement, challenges and sadness, we have had opportunities to fortify that "oneness". As my heart beats with his, I have often cried silent tears for him in times of tribulation. There have been many times in the past year that I have woken up in the middle of the night with a profound sense of sadness that I feel for the man sleeping beside me who is jobless.

As I think of the ways that I can support him, including the practical tasks like doing "job searches" or my own informal networking, I am reminded how crucial my prayers are for him. There have been times when I have prayed that God would encourage his heart, and indeed God would answer that prayer by either a call for an interview, or through support of a friend. As I learn more about prayer during this year, I realize that prayer really isn't just hurling our anxieties to God, but being in silence, contemplating God's majesty, mercy, and character. This road of an enriching prayer life is ongoing for me, but I know it is vital as I desire to care and love my husband.

In writing this book I would never want those reading this to form the perception that I am a person that always handles things well, with grace, kindness, and compassion. At times, the raggedness of my soul has spilled forth when I try to support my husband by being irritable or impatient with him and others. The reality is this author is not the perfect specimen for how to do things rightly and purely. I have fallen far short. I read recently from the *Art of Divine Contentment* by Thomas Watson that "when the sea is rough and unquiet, it casts forth nothing but foam: when the heart is discontented, it casts forth the foam of anger, impatience, and sometimes little better than blasphemy. Murmuring is nothing else but the scum which boils off from a discontented heart".[1] I have discovered that *I have* a discontented heart, and the real challenge is the fact that as much as I desire to trust God and rest in Him, I find that this is not my everyday experience. Paul Tripp expresses this struggle as he writes in a poem titled *Hearts at Rest:*

I would like to say that my heart is at rest, but I can't.
I would like to think that I always rest in God's care, but I don't.
I would love to declare that my faith is unwavering, but it isn't.

I wish it was a fact that fear is a thing of my past, but it simply isn't.

It would be nice to know that trust's struggle is over, but it isn't.

I wish I never wanted to be my own sovereign, but I do.

I want to have unbroken rest in the hand of God's love, but I don't.

I long to face difficulty without question or doubt, but I don't....[2]

I like the verse from Philippians 4:11, "I have learned to be content, whatever the circumstances" (NIV). Somehow I was deluded into thinking that this described me as I faced various circumstances in life. When life goes well and we are given a great marriage, good job, loving children, and good health, who wouldn't be "content in whatever circumstances." This year job loss has taught me that my heart is not content and it always yearns for more. Again Thomas Watson writes:

Contentment lies within the soul, and doth not

depend upon externals. Hence I gather, that outward troubles cannot hinder this blessed contentment; it is a spiritual thing, and rises from spiritual grounds; the apprehension of God's love. When there is a tempest without, there may be music within; a bee may sting through the skin, but it cannot sting to the heart; outward afflictions cannot sting to a Christian's heart, where contentment lies. Thieves may plunder us of our money and plate, but not of this pearl of contentment, unless we are willing to part with it, for it is locked up in the cabinet of the heart; the soul which is possessed of this rich treasure of contentment is like Noah in the ark, that can sing in the midst of the deluge.[3]

As I look to the year ahead on our unemployment road and how best to support my husband, I know that I desire to cultivate a contented heart. I believe that as I do, the melody of the music that rises from within will be a cause to encourage his soul as well.

Prayer:

Dear Lord,

Forgive me when I have made such feeble attempts at trusting you in this journey of unemployment. Help me to draw strength from your almighty power so that I may come alongside my husband and support him through this time. I pray also for a contented heart, one that relies in your all-sufficiency, and one that is fully captured by your love.

Thirty Days of Meditation

*I*n your unemployment journey it is important to take time a part to think, to meditate and seek God. For this chapter I wanted to offer a channel of spiritual encouragement as you face your journey as well. Each day contains a thought, saying, poem, or scripture I recorded in my journal in this past year. Many of these sayings came as I read through Oswald Chamber's devotional, *My Utmost for His Highest[1]*, and from some old Puritan prayers found in *The Valley of Vision*.[2] Take time each day to meditate, and take these words and thoughts as encouragement through your day.

Day 1: "Gaze upon the beauty of the Lord...In the time of trouble He will keep you safe."

(Psalm 27:4 NIV)

Day 2: "Our lives are to be a story that tells about His faithfulness and love."

Day 3: "The Lord is righteous in all his ways and loving toward all he has made."

(Psalm 145:17 NIV)

Day 4: "May I live to Thee

...in every Moment of my time

...in every Movement of my mind

...in every pulse of my heart"

Day 5: "The greatest injury is in having, the greatest good in the taking away."

Day 6: "My intercessor is my friend as my eyes pour out tears to God." (Job 16:20 NIV)

Day 7: "Rejoice that I am under the care of one who is too wise to err, too kind to injure..to tender to crush."

Day 8: "May his comforts cheer me in my sorrows, His strength sustain me in my trials."

Day 9: "Bring me to a happy mind that rests in Thee."

Day 10: "I rejoice to think that all things are at Thy disposal and I love to leave them there."

Day 11: "Help me to abhor that which grieves the Holy Spirit...to shun a careless way of life...to be gentle and patient towards all men."

Day 12: "Let me be what I profess, do as well as teach, live as well as hear religion."

Day 13: "You will keep in perfect peace him whose mind is steadfast, because he trusts in You."

(Isaiah 26:3 NIV)

Day 14: "Bathe my soul in rich consolations of Thy resurrection life."

Day 15: "Banish my fear...allure me into Thy presence."

Day 16: "Delight yourself in the Lord and he will give you the desires of your heart."

(Psalm 37:4 NIV)

Day 17: "Living a life of faith means never knowing where you are being led. But it does mean knowing and loving the ONE who is leading."

Day 18: "Pitch your tent in the land of hope."

(Acts: 2:28 in *The Message*)

Day 19: "Be ready for the sudden surprise visits of God."

Day 20: "...the temptation in times of waiting is to focus on the thing we are waiting for, all the obstacles that are in the way, our inability to make it happen, and all of the other people who haven't seemed to have had to wait. Along with this we rehearse to ourselves how essential the thing is and how much we are daily losing in its absence. All of this increases our feeling of helplessness, our tendency to think our situation is hopeless, and that in our judgment waiting is futile."[3]

Day 21: "We must build our faith not on fading lights but on the Light that never fades."

Day 22: "The real meaning of eternal life is a life that can face anything it has to face without wavering. If we will take this view, life will become one great romance-a glorious opportunity of seeing wonderful things all the time".[4]

Day 23: "God keeps His word even when the whole world is lying through its teeth."

(Romans 3:4 in *The Message*)

Day 24: "The Lord delights in those who fear Him who put their hope in his unfailing love."

(Psalm 147:11 NIV)

Day 25: "Come to me all you who are weary and burdened, and I will give you rest."

(Matthew 11:28 NIV)

Day 26: "I want not the favor of man to lean upon for thy favor is infinitely better."

Day 27: "Teach me to behold my creator, his ability to save, his arms outstretched, his heart big for me."

Day 28: "God does not give us overcoming life. He gives us life as we overcome."

Day 29: "Fill your mind with the thought that God is there. And once your mind is truly filled with that thought, when you experience difficulties it will be as easy as breathing for you to remember, 'My heavenly Father knows all about this!'"

Day 30: "The voyage is long, the waves high, the storms pitiless,

But my helm is held steady

Thy Word secures safe passage,

Thy grace wafts me onward,

My haven is guaranteed."

The Beat Goes on; It's a Waiting Game

*L*ast year our church's women's retreat worship team asked me if I would play the bongo drums to help in leading worship. Me? Bongo drums? Now I love music, and I sing in the church choir and know music at a very novice level, but bongo drums? I chuckled at the idea but then thought, "Why not?" My son tried to give me some tips, but mostly I was on my own, and after awhile it became fun to just feel the beat and rhythm of the music. Drums offer a pulse, or backbone to music, filling in the rhythmic steady beat. Even though this was a fun experience for me, the steady day by day beat of being unemployed is not. But indeed, the beat does go on.

As the beat goes on in our unemployment journey and job search I must admit that I really am not good at waiting. I am impatient, I want things tidy, all wrapped up in a bow, like "Okay, seek a job… get a job", now we can move on to the next thing. But mostly the job seeking journey isn't like that and it does take patience. My friend Karen who has learned well the lesson of actively waiting as she enters her second year of unemployment summarizes the "waiting" lessons as follows:

*"First, I learned to **wait expectantly**. I learned that God WILL answer my prayers, and WILL work. Knowing that God promised to work, and that He always kept His promises, helped me to wait, and to await **His working** in **His time**."*

***2 Peter 3:9** – "The Lord is not slow in keeping his promise, as some understand slowness."*

*Secondly, I learned to **wait confidently**. I knew that God would provide, even though I may not understand His timing and His* *working, I do know that He has the ability to provide – and provide beyond my ability or imagination.*

Isaiah 55:8– *"For my thoughts are not your thoughts, neither are your ways my ways," declares the LORD. "*

*Thirdly, I learned to **wait in peace**. Knowing that God promised, and that He has the ability to meet my needs, gives me tremendous peace, despite the lack of a job.*

Isaiah 26:3 – *"You will keep in perfect peace those whose minds are steadfast, because they trust in you."*

I have recently been reading Jeremiah in the Old Testament and I wrote in my journal in response to reading what God promised Jeremiah in Chapter 1.

God told Jeremiah "I am making you strong as a castle...impregnable, steel post...immovable, concrete wall...solid"

Dear Lord during this time I need this kind of strength. I am beginning to crumble. Last week ended with great disappointment for Mark. The "sure thing" was not really the "sure thing" as he looked at a great company that matched exactly what he had done at his prior company. Remember the rollercoaster? It is hard to see each potential opportunity, just drop away. Then what? ...Wait!

Paul Tripp in his devotional book "*A Shelter in the Storm*" talks about the challenge of the waiting game in our lives but gives an encouragement for the time of waiting.

"Somewhere in your life you are being called to wait. In your waiting, you are being given an opportunity to deepen and strengthen your faith. So, get up tomorrow and fill yourself with vitamins of truth. Nourish your heart with the nutrient food of the glory of God. Feed on the strength-giving meat of his

goodness, grace and love. Snack throughout the day on his power and his presence. And watch the muscles of your heart grow stronger as the days go by. Feed on the Lord and be strong!"[1]

In my closing reflections, I feel it is important to stress that no matter the life circumstance, during very dark times, one has to keep asking the question, "What is really important?" In just this past year a neighbor at age 54 died from a rare form of cancer. Another neighbor who Mark took long walks with died at age 42 leaving a wife and three year old son. All around there are people who have seemingly insurmountable trouble; a co-worker who battled breast cancer, another whose son faced a potentially life threatening heart condition placing him on the waiting list for a heart transplant, and presently a man from church facing a very aggressive cancer. What is important? I believe it is eternity and a relationship with God that adds true meaning to this sometimes hard road called life. If I am counting on a job, finances, relationships, adventures, health to give me hope, all of these could be gone in an instant. There has to be something much more solid, more lasting, and that I believe is seeking and being in a relationship with God. He has created us for a purpose to live our lives knowing Him, loving Him, and bringing glory to Him in all we do and say.

Where is our hope? A local pastor, Jeramie Rinne expresses it best as he says:

"When you go through the current financial crisis it shakes your hope. It shakes your foundation. People wonder, 'Where is our hope? Where's our country going? Where's my job going?' but when we return to the gospel, we know that God is for us: "He who did not spare His own Son, but gave Him up for us all, how will He not also, along with him, graciously give us all things? (Romans 8:32) My confidence in God's love for me is grounded in the fact that God bailed me out,

*not from financial crisis, but from having
to face his wrath. He bailed me out not at
the cost that the government paid-a trillion
dollars or so-but he bailed me out with the
price of His Son's blood. So I know that his
generosity and mercy toward me are unfath-
omable. And as I rest in the gospel and let the
gospel soak into my soul, I have confidence
that God still loves me despite the market, or
any other circumstances."[2]*

The journey of this book has ended. I wish that
I could say that Mark's journey of the job search
has also ended, but it still continues on after a year.
Pondering an ending I considered the word *inspira-
tion.* Who is it that inspires me? This question calls
to mind an Irish couple named Tom and Elizabeth,
two 80-year olds who walk through our neighborhood daily. Around noontime we will see them as
they walk around the pond we live on. But that is not
their only walk of the day for I also see them walking
on a different road at 5:00 am on my way to work.

I have been curious, "What is their story"? Recently on a 10 degree January day I went out and joined them on their walk to ask them why they walk so faithfully, no matter the weather. I was hoping that they would articulate some brilliant philosophy, or some sage old wisdom, but Tom just spoke in his thick Irish brogue, "Well, we have to get out and do something!"Isn't that the truth? Simple. It is just getting out, putting one foot in front of the other, walking this road called unemployment. Yes, the steady beat rings in our ears, "I need a job, I need a job," and we wonder when there will be silence again...but wait, God will show that He is faithful. In a card given to Mark recently to encourage him the person wrote a phrase, "thank you for your long obedience in the same direction." That is the call to all of us to continue in obedience, putting one foot in front of the other like Tom and Elizabeth, a steady pace, faithfully every day.

Prayer:

Dear Lord,

Help us to continue on this road of unemployment with a steady confident pace, counting out the continual beat of how you have shown yourself faithful. It is with joy and hope that we look forward to the days ahead, for with you we will win. Help us to wait expectantly, confidently and in peace, knowing you will provide the right job in your time.

Mark the Hiker....someday the John Muir Trail!

End Notes

Book cover design, Deborah Sovinee:
www.inkythumb.com

Introduction
[1]Rich Lowry, "An Unemployment Catastrophe",
(June 10, 2011); *National Review*;
http://www.nationalreview.com/articles/269296
(Accessed on September 18, 2011)

God's Provision
[1]Learn about COBRA:
http://www.ehealthinsurance.com/cobra-insura
(Accessed October 1, 2011)

[2]Michael Melcher," What To Do When You Lose
Your Job", (March 5, 2009); *New York Times*,
The Opinion Pages; http://roomfordebate.blogs.
nytimes.com/2009 (Accessed September 22, 2011)

The New Norm
[1]Thomas O. Chisholm, *"Great is thy Faithfulness"*

Wisdom from Some Old Books

[1]Bernie Powell, "Alternate Education", *The Family Postman*, January 2011.(Used by permission)

[2]Mark Nevens, "Personal Testimony", *The Family Postman*, October 2011.(Used by permission)

[3-9]Thomas Boston, *The Crook in the Lot* (First published in 18th Century) (Reprinted: Morgan, PA. Soli Deo Gloria Publications, 2001) (pages: 3-4, 9, 31, 49-50, 55, 67)

The Roller Coaster

[1]Joel Schofield, *Carousel*: www.joelschofieldmusic.com. (Used by permission)

[2]Rich Lowry, "An Unemployment Catastrophe", (June 10, 2011); *National Review*; http://www.nationalreview.com/articles/269296 (Accessed on September 18, 2011)

[3]Holmes and Rahe Stress Scale: http://en.wikipedia.org/wiki/Holmes_and_Rahe (Accessed September 22, 2011)

The Scarlett "U"

[1]Tony Pugh, "Is U.S. Losing Patience with Jobless?" *The Fresno Bee*, 4 September 2011.

[2]Rich Lowry, "An Unemployment Catastrophe", (June 10, 2011); *National Review*; http://www.nationalreview.com/articles/269296 (Accessed on September 18, 2011)

[3]The script for the movie *The Company Men* by John Wells can be found at http://twcawards.com/assets/downloads/pdf/the-company-men.pdf (Accessed on October 1, 2011)

Merry Heart Moments
[1]Louise Carey, *The Hedge People* (Beacon Hill Press, 2009), p. 5.

[2]http://igbok.com (Accessed on September 22, 2011)

Ten Truths for the Journey
[1-3,5,8-12]Oswald Chambers, *My Utmost for His Highest* (Discovery House Publishers, 1992), Devotionals: June 18, June 27, July 4, July 16, July 20, July 28, August 2, August 6, August 12

[4]Steve McVey, *Walking in the Will of God* (Harvest House Publishers, 2009), p. 126.

[6]Raymond Edman, *The Disciplines of Life* (Scripture Press Foundation, 1948), p. 37.

[7]William Bathurst, *"O, For a Faith That Will Not Shrink"*

If I Ran the Zoo
[1]Theodor S. Giesel (Dr. Seuss), *If I Ran the Zoo* (Random House, 1950), p. 2.

[2]The script for the movie *The Company Men* by John Wells can be found at http://twcawards.com/assets/downloads/pdf/the-company-men.pdf (Accessed on October 1, 2011)

[3]http://en.wikipedia.org/wiki/Aaron_Feurstein (Accessed on October 10, 2011)

[4-5]Charles Kelleher Harris, "Rising From The Ashes" *The Enterprise*, 26 September 2011. Pgs.1, 4.

[6]Thomas J. Peters and Robert H. Waterman, Jr., *In Search of Excellence* (New York: Harper & Row, 1982), p. 13

A Wife's Reflections

[1,3]Thomas Watson, *The Art of Divine Contentment* (Glasgow, U.K., no date), Kindle Edition. Loc. 533-537; 580-590.

[2]Paul David Tripp, *A Shelter in the Time of Storm* (Crossway Books, 2009), p 144-146.

Thirty Days of Meditation

[1]Oswald Chambers, *My Utmost for His Highest* (Discovery House Publishers, 1992), Devotionals: April 18, April 22, March 19, May 8, July 16, August 2.

[2]Edited by Arthur Bennett, *The Valley of Vision* (The Banner of Truth Trust, Versa Press, 2005), Pgs: 11, 18, 24, 30, 36, 37, 58, 59, 61, 63, 110, 152.

[3]Paul David Tripp, *A Shelter in the Time of Storm* (Crossway Books, 2009), p. 48.

[4]Steve McVey, *Walking in the Will of God* (Harvest House Publishers, 2009), p. 126.

The Beat Goes on: It's a Waiting Game

[1]Paul David Tripp, *A Shelter in the Time of Storm* (Crossway Books, 2009), p. 159.

[2]Jeramie Rinne, "The Gospel is the Christian Life" *Gordon-Conwell Theological Seminary Annual Report*, 2011, p. 23.

nmsc

nmschofield@hotmail.com

CPSIA information can be obtained at www.ICGtesting.com
Printed in the USA
BVOW062038150512

290306BV00001B/1/P